Catholic Update
guide to
Confirmation

MARY CAROL KENDZIA
Series Editor

ST. ANTHONY MESSENGER PRESS
Cincinnati, Ohio

RESCRIPT
In accord with the *Code of Canon Law,* I hereby grant the Imprimatur
("Permission to Publish") to
Catholic Update Guide to Confirmation

Most Reverend Joseph R. Binzer
Vicar General and Auxiliary Bishop
Archdiocese of Cincinnati
Cincinnati, Ohio
October 21, 2011

Scripture passages have been taken from *New Revised Standard Version Bible,* copyright ©1989 by the Division of Christian Education of the National Council of the Churches of Christ in the U.S.A., and used by permission. All rights reserved.

Cover and book design by Mark Sullivan. Cover image © Fotolia | Irochka

LIBRARY OF CONGRESS CATALOGING-IN-PUBLICATION DATA
Catholic update guide to confirmation / Mary Carol Kendzia, series editor.
p. cm.
ISBN 978-1-61636-239-3 (alk. paper)
1. Confirmation—Catholic Church. 2. Catholic Church—Doctrines. I. Kendzia,
Mary Carol.
BX2210.C38 2012
234'.162—dc23

2011042889

ISBN 978-1-61636-239-3

Copyright ©2012, St. Anthony Messenger Press.
All rights reserved.

Published by St. Anthony Messenger Press
28 W. Liberty St.
Cincinnati, OH 45202
www.AmericanCatholic.org
www.SAMPBooks.org

Printed in the United States of America.
Printed on acid-free paper.
12 13 14 15 16   5 4 3 2

Contents

About This Series

The Catholic Update guides take the best material from our best-selling newsletters and videos to bring you up-to-the-minute resources for your faith. Topically arranged for these books, the words you'll find in these pages are the same clear, concise, authoritative information you've come to expect from the nation's most trusted faith formation series. Plus, we've designed this series with a practical focus—giving the "what," "why," and "how to" for the people in the pews.

The series takes the topics most relevant to parish life— for example, the Mass, sacraments, Scripture, the liturgical year— and draws them out in a fresh and straightforward way. The books can be read by individuals or used in a study group. They are an invaluable resource for sacramental preparation, RCIA participants, faith formation, and liturgical ministry training, and are a great tool for everyday Catholics who want to brush up on the basics.

The content for the series comes from noted authors such as Thomas Richstatter, O.F.M., Lawrence Mick, Leonard Foley, O.F.M., Carol Luebering, William H. Shannon, and others. Their theology and approach is grounded in Catholic practice and tradition, while mindful of current Church practice and teaching. We blend each author's style and approach into a voice that is clear, unified, and eminently readable.

Enrich your knowledge and practice of the Catholic faith with the helpful topics in the Catholic Update Guide series.

Mary Carol Kendzia
Series Editor

Introduction

Confirmation is one of the three so-called "sacraments of initiation." Through baptism, confirmation, and Eucharist a person is born again, strengthened, and nourished in order to live fully the Christian life. The *Catechism of the Catholic Church (CCC)* calls these three sacraments "the foundations of every Christian life" (#1212). Pope Paul VI said that these sacraments give "in increasing measure the treasures of the divine life," and described them as the means by which the faithful come to share in the nature of God.

The sacraments of baptism and Eucharist have a rich theology. The Church's *Code of Canon Law* insists that baptism is the gateway to the other sacraments and is necessary for salvation. Through baptism, Canon 849 explains, "men and women are freed from sin, are reborn as children of God, and, configured to

Christ by an indelible character, are incorporated in to the Church."

The theological explanation of confirmation, however, is less passionate, more prosaic. Canon 879 says this sacrament strengthens the baptized, obliges them to give witness to and defend the faith, imprints a character, and enriches them on their continuing path of Christian initiation by the gift of the Holy Spirit.

The very wording of Canon 879 suggests that there are differing theologies or explanations of the sacrament. These differences are understandable in light of its historical development and the variety of ways in which it has been administered. The Latin Rite bishops of the United States, for example, do not agree on the most appropriate age for a young person to be confirmed; the norm in the United States is "between the age of discretion and about sixteen years," allowing variations in dioceses across the country.

The *Catholic Update Guide to Confirmation* will review the what, why, and how of the sacrament. Although some theologians and liturgists have complained that "confirmation is a sacrament in search of a theology," there is more than sufficient agreement among the Catholic faithful that those who have been baptized should continue on the path of Christian initiation through this sacrament.

CHAPTER ONE

What Is Confirmation?

The Second Vatican Council (1962–1965) ordered the revision of the rites for baptism and confirmation. As a result the Church has the Rite of Christian Initiation of Adults (RCIA) and a baptismal ritual for infants—both of which emphasize that baptism is the first step of initiation into the fullness of the Christian community. The revised Rite of Confirmation emphasizes its relationship to baptism, seeing it as stage two of the initiation begun in baptism.

In this chapter we will look first at the ritual for confirmation, and then let Fr. Thomas Richstatter, O.F.M., describe the nature of confirmation and develop its intimate connection to baptism. His analysis explores the history of the sacrament and reveals why our understanding of confirmation cannot be separated from our baptismal promises.

The Rite of Confirmation

The Rite of Confirmation is extraordinarily simple. It normally includes a renewal of baptismal promises, the laying on of hands, the anointing with the oil of chrism, and a blessing.

The usual minister of the sacrament is a bishop, but priests are routinely authorized to administer confirmation. Those to be confirmed (often called the confirmandi) formally renew the promises they made in baptism. They are asked if they renounce Satan and profess the basic beliefs of the Church.

Next, the bishop asks all who are present to pray for those about to be confirmed, and then extends his hands over the confirmandi and asks God to send the Holy Spirit upon them and give them "the spirit of wisdom and understanding, the spirit of right judgment and courage, the spirit of knowledge and reverence." He ends his prayer by asking the Father to fill the confirmandi "with the spirit of wonder and awe."

Finally the bishop individually anoints the confirmandi with a specially blessed oil called chrism, making the sign of the cross on each candidate's forehead, saying as he does, "Be sealed with the Gift of the Holy Spirit." Each newly confirmed replies, "Amen." The bishop then says (perhaps shaking the hand of the newly confirmed as he does so), "Peace be with you." The newly confirmed responds, "And also with you."

During the time of preparation for receiving confirmation, each of the confirmandi chooses a saint to model, someone who can serve as an inspiration, and takes his or her name. Each of the confirmandi also chooses a baptized and confirmed Catholic to act as sponsor, someone who will act as an earthly model of Christian life. The sponsor may be the same person who served as sponsor or godparent for baptism.

Ordinarily confirmation takes place during Mass. If the confirmandi have been enrolled in the RCIA (Rite of Christian Initiation of Adults) program, confirmation is conferred during the Easter Vigil ceremonies, on the night before Easter Sunday.

A Sacrament of Initiation

Franciscan friar Thomas Richstatter remembers his own confirmation and tells us a little more about the sacrament: I was a ten-year-old fourth grader at St. Anthony School in Wichita, Kansas. Today, Catholics often associate confirmation with high school or even junior high. In fact, in a small but increasing number of parishes, children are being confirmed at a much younger age, before they receive First Communion. Each year at the Easter Vigil we see adult converts receiving confirmation immediately after their baptism. Catholics of the Roman Rite may be surprised to learn that in most Eastern Rites even infants are confirmed at baptism.

The sacrament of confirmation confers the Holy Spirit; but with so many different ways in which confirmation is celebrated, we might well ask why there is such a wide variety in styles of celebration. What is confirmation? Is it a sacrament of "Christian maturity" when given to infants? Does it make children "soldiers of Christ"? Is the Spirit given at confirmation somehow different from the Holy Spirit given at baptism? Are these even the right questions to ask?

The best way to understand confirmation is to see it standing between baptism and Eucharist as part of the Rites of Christian Initiation. This is the approach taken by the *Catechism of the Catholic Church*, which treats confirmation under the heading "Sacraments of Christian Initiation," and insists that the unity of baptism, confirmation, and Eucharist "must be safeguarded."

Recent historical investigations into the origins of our sacramental rituals reveal a rich diversity in the early Church. It is difficult to trace with precision how the Church, acting under the direction of the Holy Spirit, elaborated the sacramental rituals instituted by Christ. But in its simplest outline, these rituals developed within the framework of a dinner invitation.

In prophecy and parable Jesus spoke of the Kingdom of God as a banquet—a great eating together. "I tell you, many will come from east and west and will eat with Abraham and Isaac and Jacob in the kingdom of heaven" (Matthew 8:11). God has invited the whole human family to join in a great heavenly banquet. We respond to this invitation through the Sacraments of Initiation.

An Analogy: Washing, Drying, Eating

Consider for a moment what you do when you are invited out to eat. Let's say that you have been out working in the garden and a friend calls and asks if you would like to come over for dinner and you accept the invitation. What happens next? Probably, three things: First, you would take off your work clothes and wash up, perhaps taking a shower or a bath. Second, you would dry off and put on clean clothes. And third, you would go over to your friend's house and eat.

This sequence of events is perhaps the simplest way to understand the sacraments of initiation. God has invited each of us to dine with Christ at the eucharistic banquet. When we come to this table for the first time, we put off the "old self" (see, for example, Romans 6:6; Ephesians 4:22; and Colossians 3:9) and wash away the stain of original sin. This is the sacramental bath of baptism. Second, we dry off. In the first and second centuries, however, Romans would rub their bodies with oil after bathing to moisturize the skin as it dried. In our sacramental system the bath of baptism is followed by the oil of confirmation. And, third, clothed with the Holy Spirit, we are invited to the eucharistic table.

This three-step sequence can help us understand some of the contemporary development and understanding of the sacraments of initiation, for example, the sequence of the three sacraments when they are celebrated together in our parishes at the Easter Vigil. Of course, the historical development of the rites is much more complex, especially the development of the rite we call confirmation.

We do not find much written specifically about confirmation in the early Church, because when the early Christian authors wrote about baptism they often implied both the water bath and the anointing with oil—what today we call baptism and confirmation. For example, if you invited me out to eat and I said, "Let me wash up first, and then we'll go," by "washing up" I would imply both the washing and the drying; there would be no need to specifically mention the "drying off" (or anointing, if we were ancient Romans).

Baptism and confirmation are also intimately related in another way. When we take a bath, we get clean by washing off the dirt. We can speak of "getting clean" and we can speak of "washing off dirt" but, actually, removing "dirtiness" and receiving "cleanliness" go together. They are two ways of looking at one action. In a similar way, early Church writers described baptism with the "washing off" metaphors and spoke of confirmation with the "getting clean" metaphors. Baptism washes away all sin, original and actual; and confirmation gives us the grace and presence of the Holy Spirit. Of course, taking away sin and being filled with grace are but two ways of speaking of the same action, something like "washing off" and "getting clean." The two actions go together even if we call them by the different names of baptism and confirmation.

This analogy of "washing up, drying off, going to eat" works especially well for baptism, confirmation, and Eucharist when they are celebrated in that sequence—as they were in the early Church, and as they are today in most of the non-Roman Rites of the Catholic Church, and as they are in the Roman Catholic Church for adults and children of catechetical age at the Easter Vigil.

A Break in the Link

The analogy does not fit as well, however, when confirmation is separated from baptism by a number of years, and especially when it comes after Eucharist rather than before—as is usually the case with children baptized as infants in the Roman Catholic Church.

How did confirmation come to be separated from baptism? In the early Church, the bishop or *episcopos* ("overseer") was the original minister of all the sacraments. In the fourth century, when priests or *presbyteros* ("elder") began to baptize and preside at the Eucharist, the anointing after baptism which conferred the Holy Spirit began to be reserved to the bishop in those churches that followed the liturgical customs of Rome. Because the dioceses of central Italy were very small, this was usually a separation of only a few weeks or months. But as the customs of Rome were extended to the whole Western Church, the separation between the two parts of the rite increased from weeks to years.

Although the confirmation part of initiation came to be delayed in the Western Church, Eucharist remained an integral part of the ceremony. While initiation by baptism, confirmation, and Eucharist continued to be the norm in the East, infants, children, and adult converts in the West received only baptism and Eucharist at the same time. Infants received their First Communion at baptism until about the twelfth century, when changing eucharistic understanding and devotion caused pastors to worry that infants could not have the necessary reverence to receive the Eucharist.

Furthermore, to avoid any danger that the infant might "spit up" the consecrated host, infants began to be given only the Precious Blood at Communion time. (Some years ago when I was studying in Egypt, with my limited American understanding of the world and the Church, I first thought it very strange to see infants in the Coptic churches being brought up for Communion. With parents holding the infants in front of him, the priest would dip his little finger into the consecrated wine and place it on the lips of the infant.)

When, in the twelfth and thirteenth centuries, Communion from the cup was generally withdrawn from the laity in the Roman Church, it was also denied to infants. However, since infants did not receive the consecrated bread, this in effect meant that they no longer received Communion at each Eucharist from the time of their baptism and had to wait for their First Communion. Communion was delayed until after a period of catechetical formation, often at the age of fourteen or fifteen.

Usually during the course of these fourteen or fifteen years, the bishop had the opportunity to visit the parish or the parents had the opportunity to bring the child to the cathedral, and so most of these children receiving First Communion had already been confirmed. Even though the sacraments of initiation were spread out over a number of years, the sequence remained baptism, confirmation, Eucharist.

In 1906 Pope Pius X encouraged children as young as six or seven to receive the Eucharist. While lowering the age for First Communion had many positive benefits, it also caused many children to receive Eucharist before confirmation. The explanation of baptism, confirmation, and Eucharist as "washing up, drying off, and going to eat" didn't fit any more because we "go out to eat" several years before we "dry off."

As confirmation became separated from baptism by a number of years, teachers, and preachers began to speak of the meaning of confirmation apart from the meaning of baptism. Confirmation began to be described as a sacrament of "strengthening." The embrace of welcome and "kiss of peace" (which had become a "love pat" in the case of infants) now became a "slap on the cheek" to remind those being confirmed that they had become "soldiers for Christ." Other explanations of confirmation were developed that were especially suited to needs of the adolescents receiving the sacrament.

RCIA: A New Look

In the years preceding the Second Vatican Council, Church leaders looked carefully at the current state of our initiation rites in light of this long and rather complicated history, and they decided that some changes in emphasis should be made to better adapt these sacraments to the pastoral needs of the contemporary Church. Following the discussion of these matters at the council, the Church published four documents: *Christian Initiation: General Introduction*, *Rite of Baptism for Children*, *Rite of Confirmation*, and *Rite of Christian Initiation of Adults*, which has come to be known by its initials, RCIA. Each of these revised rites, and especially the RCIA, has had a profound effect on Church life in the United States.

The RCIA restores the order of baptism-confirmation-Eucharist and emphasizes the interconnectedness of these three sacraments (as we saw above: washing up, drying off, and going to eat). These rites are neither separate nor are they static; they are part of an ongoing process. The RCIA speaks of our faith journey. And this journey does not end at baptism or First Communion, or even at confirmation, but continues throughout our Christian life. The sacraments of initiation are a continual invitation to continued conversion.

This faith journey is not merely a matter of learning about the faith, not merely instruction, but also a true conversion process. It involves the whole life of the candidate and the whole life of the Church. These sacraments are not private events. They affect the whole Church. Conversion takes place in community. Conversion implies initiation into that community, initiation into the body of Christ.

In 2000 the bishops of the United States published *Journey to the Fullness of Life: A Report on the Implementation of the Rite of Christian Initiation of Adults in the United States*. The results of this comprehensive study make it clear that the RCIA is renewing the life of the Church in the United States, say the bishops. "This study also affirms that faith formation is a lifelong process.... The image of a journey is one that is often used in reference to the RCIA and that fits with an understanding of catechesis/adult faith formation as a lifelong process." Again and again the report stresses that the initiation of catechumens is a "gradual process that takes place within the community of the faithful" (http://old.usccb.org/evangelization/journey).

Fr. Richstatter's remembrance of his confirmation and his analysis of the sacraments of initiation affirm the communal nature of these sacraments and put the initiated squarely in the mission and ministry of the Church: Theologian Karl Rahner saw in baptism and confirmation the sacramental basis for the position of the laypeople in the Church. Through these sacraments a person receives the divine call and becomes a contributing member in the work of the Church. The Church is composed of the faithful, or as the Second Vatican Council called them, "the holy people of God." Bishops, priests, deacons, and members of religious communities are members of the people of God long before they begin their special ministries.

Vatican II's Constitution on the Church (*Lumen Gentium*) makes it clear that through baptism and confirmation the faithful have an obligation to profess their faith and are strictly obliged to spread the faith by word and deed (cf. *Lumen Gentium*, 11). All the holy people of God share in Christ's priestly and prophetic office.

Rahner acknowledged that as a dogmatic theologian he found it difficult to distinguish between baptism and confirmation regarding their meaning and their effects. He considered them taken together as constituting a single initiation into becoming Christian. And as a result the confirmed Christian, whether lay or cleric, is in the position of one who has a mission and a task. The baptized/confirmed Christian, Rahner said, has a personal responsibility for the world in virtue of his initiation into the Christian faith.

Questions for Reflection

1. Why are we asked to choose a saint's name for confirmation? Why do we need to choose a sponsor?

2. How does the RCIA program affirm the intimate relationship between baptism and confirmation?

3. As baptized and confirmed Christians we are members of the "community of the faithful." Are we an inviting community? What makes people want to join us?

CHAPTER TWO

Why Do We Receive Confirmation?

The New Testament, especially Acts 8:14–17 and 19:1–6, indicates that at least in some settings there were two distinct rituals even in the first days of the Church: baptism and the laying on of hands. The gesture of imposing hands in these two instances was connected with the subsequent manifestation of the Holy Spirit. As history shows, Christian initiation began with a twofold ritual (baptism and imposition of hands); over time the two rituals were separated. It is our understanding that the Holy Spirit comes to strengthen the baptized, and further enriches the confirmed.

In this chapter Dr. Joseph Martos explains why one should receive the sacrament of confirmation. Then Thomas Richstatter, O.F.M., complements that explanation by stressing the intimate link between confirmation and the other two sacraments of initiation.

Why Should We Be Confirmed?

It's been a long time, Dr. Martos reflects, but I can remember my confirmation well. The forty of us were lined up in the schoolyard on a cold day, our red "graduation" robes blowing in the wind. We were only in the fifth grade, but we were allowed to wear the robes for confirmation—red being the color the Church uses to represent the Holy Spirit. We felt very grown-up, and very proud.

An hour later, as far as I could tell, it was over. We had been anointed with oil on the forehead and slapped lightly on the cheek. In those days, that "slap" told us that we had to be "soldiers of Christ," ready to suffer for our faith. We had sung "Come, Holy Ghost," and the bishop had prayed over us and put his hand on our head. I felt like I had been ordained or surely something as important and official as that.

I look back on that day of years ago and ask myself, what difference did it make? It was a nice ceremony—almost like a parade or a welcome-home celebration. And of course there was the party afterward and the confirmation presents. But really, I didn't understand how much of a welcome it was—and to what!

My wife tells me that, for her, the sacrament did make a big difference right away. I was glad to hear that on her confirmation day she felt the love and power of God in a special way. She began to pray more, and attended Mass on weekdays. She made a constant effort to be more helpful at home, to be more polite to her parents, and to be less quarrelsome with her sisters—and she felt the grace within her to succeed.

Connecting the Present to the Past

To help me know why we do what we do now in the Church, I like to recall our Church history and tradition. In the early days of the Church, many Christians felt the Holy Spirit come into their life through the "laying on of hands," as it was called then. A leader of the Christian community would lay his hands on those who had been baptized and pray for the Holy Spirit to come down into them. This practice seems to have been a forerunner of the official sacrament that we now call confirmation. Afterward, these new Christians would spontaneously be inspired to praise God aloud and pray in languages they hadn't known before.

Today, some Christians called Pentecostals or charismatics (including Catholics) testify that they have had this same experience—being "baptized in the Spirit," as they call it. It is not the same as the sacrament of confirmation, but it is a practice that seems to make them more receptive to the presence of the Holy Spirit. They feel changed inside, and charged with a spiritual energy that they never had before.

The way confirmation is celebrated in the Church today is a reminder of that early Christian practice, although the bishop no longer lays his hands directly on the heads of those who are being confirmed. During the ceremony, the bishop extends his hands over the candidates and prays:

> All-powerful God, Father of our Lord Jesus Christ, by water and the Holy Spirit you freed your sons and daughters from sin and gave them new life. Send your Holy Spirit upon them to be their helper and guide. Give them the spirit of wisdom and understanding, the spirit of right judgment and courage, the spirit of knowledge and reverence. Fill them with the spirit of wonder and awe in your presence.

Earlier in the ceremony, to prepare them for this moment, the bishop asked the candidates to renew the promises that their parents made for them at baptism. He went over each of the major points of the Creed we say every Sunday at Mass and asked the candidates whether they believe in the Fatherhood of God, the Lordship of Christ, the work of the Holy Spirit, and other teachings of the Church.

When the candidates respond to these statements of faith, they do so in a group, as part of the confirmation ceremony. They all give the same outward response, but inwardly their responses can differ in emotional intensity. Some may reaffirm their faith with all their heart, and they may open themselves up to a deeper and more mature awareness of the Holy Spirit's presence in their life. Others may feel absolutely no change of heart as they go through the confirmation ceremony. Most people's experience probably falls somewhere in between these two extremes.

Different experiences of confirmation are matched by different responses to the sacrament and its graces. In talking about my wife, I said that she not only felt something different at her confirmation, but she also behaved differently afterwards. On the other hand, I don't remember behaving any differently right after I was confirmed, although I can honestly say that if I weren't a confirmed Christian I might have lived my life very differently over the years.

And I'm sure that there are people whose confirmation has never, ever made any difference whatsoever in their life. Then again, most people fall somewhere between the two extremes.

The Origins of the Sacrament

With these widely differing responses to confirmation, why do we have it at all? What can we expect? Where did it come from?

In the earliest days of Christianity (we learn about them from the New Testament, especially from the Epistles of St. Paul and the Acts of the Apostles), adults became members of the Church through both a water baptism and a laying-on of hands. For many converts, becoming a Christian meant giving up sinful habits and beginning a new life. They felt a great spiritual energy to live differently from the majority of people around them.

Centuries after the apostles, when almost everyone in the Roman Empire was Christian, most people no longer experienced such dramatic change in their life at confirmation. In the fourth century, for example, St. Augustine wrote, "Who in the present day expects that those on whom hands are laid for the bestowal of the Spirit will suddenly begin speaking in tongues?" In other words, only a few hundred years away from the apostles, those charismatic gifts I mentioned earlier had all but disappeared. Becoming a Christian by that time meant living like everybody else and seldom suffering or even feeling uncomfortable.

As years passed, the laying-on of hands by the bishop was changed to an anointing with oil, since in the Scriptures anointing is often associated with the reception of God's Spirit. And, some years after that, the full ceremony of Christian initiation into the Church was divided into two parts: baptism with water by a priest, and anointing with oil by a bishop. This happened because the bishop could not always be present at everyone's baptism, and yet he wanted to personally receive every new Christian into full membership in the Church. After a while, this second part of Christian initiation became a completely separate ritual called confirmation.

Eventually it turned out that, while all Christians were baptized, few were confirmed. One reason for this was that every parish had a priest but bishops were few and far between, just as today.

What Difference Can Confirmation Make?

Seeing how the practice of confirmation has differed widely down through the centuries, even falling into long periods of disuse, a more radical question can creep into our mind: Why keep up the practice of confirmation at all?

One obvious answer is that confirmation is a part of our tradition. It is a part of the Catholic heritage. By continuing the practice of confirmation we show that we accept and continue that heritage.

Still, is this enough? Of course not. Just because we have always confirmed in some way is not a good enough reason for continuing to do it today. There must be more reasons than that.

One important reason is that confirmation can make a real difference in the lives of young people. It can give them a chance to think about their baptism and about what it means to be a Christian. When they were baptized as infants, they didn't know what was happening. Now, when they are older, they have a chance to reaffirm their membership in the Church and to say their own "I do" to their baptismal promises.

So confirmation can indeed make a difference in our lives. It can have the effect of a special spiritual awakening, as it had for my wife. Or it can have the effect of being a special reminder of our commitment to Christ and to the Church, as it was for me. A lot depends on each individual and on the circumstances surrounding their own confirmation.

What Difference Do You Want It to Make?

Many of us were confirmed before we were ready to make this serious commitment. We said we were willing to be confirmed Christians, and the bishop anointed us with the sign of Christ's cross.

In some ways, it's a question of maturity. If you've already been confirmed, you're older now than you were then. You've recited the Creed, a statement of your beliefs, Sunday after Sunday at Mass. You've learned more about the meaning of your faith. But have you taken the time to make your Christian living more mature as well? Does the meaning your head already knows take shape in actions from your heart?

God always offers you the grace to live up to your baptismal promises and to the commitment that your parents made for you at baptism. So the important question is this: What difference do you allow the sacrament of confirmation to make in your life? If confirmation does not seem to have the expected or desired effect, it is not that God has in any way failed you.

When you were confirmed, you renewed the promises that your parents made for you at your baptism: to believe in God, to be a member of the Church, to avoid sin and lead a moral life. As you are probably aware, there's a lot packed into those simple phrases. There's also a lot of commitment that is demanded of you if you take them seriously.

And how seriously do you take these promises? I believe that being a Christian, especially a confirmed Christian, should make a noticeable difference in a person's life. Jesus once said, "Not everyone who says to me, 'Lord, Lord,' will enter the kingdom of heaven, but only one who does the will of my Father in heaven" (Matthew 7:21). He meant that saying the words was not enough; choosing to know and do God's will was necessary. Being a confirmed Christian, like being a confirmed soccer player or a confirmed music lover, is a matter of deeds, not words.

How to Make It Matter

You may honestly believe that being a confirmed Christian ought to make a difference in your life, but you don't know how to go about making this change. Or you may realize that growing toward Christian maturity ought to have a greater impact on your life, but you're not sure what it should be. Here are a few practical suggestions about living up to the potential inherent in the sacrament of confirmation—no matter what your age:

1. Learn more about what it means to be a Christian. Read the Gospels (Matthew 5—7 is a good place to begin) to see what Jesus asks of his followers. Find a book on how to live the Christian life (there are lots of them) and find one area where you might make an improvement. Ask someone whose faith you admire (age doesn't matter) how he or she tries to live a Christian life.

2. Think about yourself, your own hopes and ambitions, your own values and ideals. Take the time to write them down. Then ask yourself how they stack up against what you find in the Gospels and what you learn about living up to the teachings of Christ. Compare your own goals in life and your own personal behavior in the light of what it means to be a confirmed Christian.

3. If you find differences between the way you are and the way you think a Christian should be, make some honest judgments about which way you want to go. This kind of self-examination is not easy, but the results are very rewarding. You may find yourself faced with some difficult choices, but it is up to you to make these choices. No one else can make them for you.

4. If you want to change your goals or behavior as a result of what you find out about yourself, be practical about it. Don't try to change everything at once. Pray about it, and ask for guidance from someone you respect. And don't try to do it alone. When you feel discouraged, remember change is a lifelong task. Get in touch with other people in your parish or school who seem to be taking their Christian commitment seriously. Confirmation can and does make a difference—if you allow, even welcome, such change.

Confirmation as the Sacrament of the Spirit

Fr. Richstatter complements Dr. Martos's explanation of why a baptized person should be confirmed. He focuses our attention on the power that comes in the Holy Spirit. Every Christian knows it is difficult to follow Christ faithfully. Jesus consoled his disciples at the Last Supper, promising them an Advocate, a Spirit of truth, to guide them (see John 16). It is biblical tradition and Church teaching that the Spirit comes in power through the laying on of hands.

Richstatter notes that in early Church documents we do not find much written about confirmation because it was considered part of baptism. In these documents the authors, when writing about baptism, often meant both baptism and confirmation, both the water bath and the anointing with oil.

We can call one action baptism and the other confirmation. We can even celebrate them at two different times in a person's faith journey, but to understand them correctly we must view them together. It is one and the same Holy Spirit celebrated at baptism, confirmation and Eucharist.

Each sacrament is both sign and words. To understand confirmation, the sacrament of the Spirit, look at the words which accompany the Sacraments of Initiation.

At baptism, we hear of the role of the Holy Spirit in the prayer over the baptismal water:

Father, look now with love on your Church,
and unseal for her the fountain of baptism.
By the power of the Spirit
give to the water of this font
the grace of your Son...
cleanse [those to be baptized] from sin in a new birth of
    innocence
by water and the Spirit.

At confirmation, we learn the implications of this new life in the
Holy Spirit:

All-powerful God,
Father of our Lord Jesus Christ,
by water and the Holy Spirit
you freed your sons and daughters from sin
And gave them new life.
Send your Holy Spirit upon them
to be their Helper and Guide.
Give them the spirit of wisdom and understanding,
the spirit of right judgment and courage,
the spirit of knowledge and reverence.
Fill them with the spirit of wonder and awe in your presence.

This prayer names the traditional seven gifts of the Holy Spirit.
The biblical origin of these seven gifts is found in Isaiah (11:1–3)
where he is foretelling the qualities of the Messiah:

A shoot shall come out from the stump of Jesse,
  and a branch shall grow out of his roots.
The spirit of the LORD shall rest on him,
  the spirit of wisdom and understanding,
  the spirit of counsel and might,
  the spirit of knowledge and the fear of the LORD.
His delight shall be in the fear of the LORD.

[The ancient Greek and Latin translations of this passage read "piety" for "fear of the Lord" in line six; this gives us our traditional seven gifts of the Holy Spirit.]

These seven gifts are the signs that the Messiah will be guided by the Spirit. The relation of these gifts to the sacrament of confirmation becomes clear when we remember that the word *Messiah* (*Christos* in Greek) means "anointed." Jesus was anointed, filled with the Holy Spirit at his baptism. At confirmation we are anointed with the Holy Spirit. Throughout the Gospels we see how these seven gifts form Jesus' personality. They are characteristic of his activity.

Consider the wisdom expressed in his parables; his understanding of the poor and the sick; his right judgment when tested by the Pharisees; his courage to continue the journey to Jerusalem where he surmised what fate awaited him; his knowledge of God's will; his reverence for his heavenly Father; his awe before the wonders of creation—the lilies of the field, the birds of the air.

The seven gifts of the Holy Spirit are the manifestation of the divine power active in the life of Jesus of Nazareth.

In baptism, our sins are washed away and we come up from the water bath to be clothed in a new garment. Putting on the baptismal garment is a visible symbol of the invisible reality of "putting on Christ." When we are anointed with oil in confirmation, it is a visible symbol of the invisible reality of being anointed with the Spirit, being "Christ-ed" or "messiah-ed." We put on Christ, and the sevenfold gifts of the Spirit become our gifts. We pray that the qualities of the Messiah take root in us and become our qualities so that we may become signs of God's presence in the world.

At the actual anointing during confirmation we hear the words: "[Name], be sealed with the gift of the Holy Spirit." Here the gift referred to is the Holy Spirit. We are sealed with the gift of (that is, the gift which is) the Holy Spirit. The Holy Spirit is God's "first fruits for those who believe" (Eucharistic Prayer IV).

Confirmation Leads to Eucharist

"The holy Eucharist completes Christian initiation" (*CCC*, #1322). With our sins washed away and being clothed in the Spirit, we are led to the banquet table of the Eucharist. The ancient Eucharistic Prayer II expresses the role of the Holy Spirit more clearly than the traditional Roman Canon (Eucharistic Prayer I). Although the words vary according to the prayer, at each

Eucharist we ask God: "Make holy, therefore, these gifts, we pray, by sending down your Spirit upon them like the dewfall...that, partaking of the Body and Blood of Christ, we may be gathered into one by the Holy Spirit" (Eucharistic Prayer II).

At each Eucharist we ask the Holy Spirit to do two things: first, to change the bread and wine into the sacred Body and Blood of Christ; and, second, to change us—those who eat and drink the sacred bread and wine—into the sacred Body and Blood of Christ. The saying, "You are what you eat," certainly holds true here. As St. Augustine reminded his fourth-century audience: "If then you are the body of Christ and his members, it is your sacrament that reposes on the altar of the Lord.... Be what you see and receive what you are" and "There you are on the table, and there you are in the chalice."

As Catholics, we are proud of our tradition of reverence for the Body and Blood of Christ, which by faith we perceive as really present in the action of the Spirit changing the bread and wine. This same Spirit challenges us to the often more difficult reverence for the body of Christ which, by faith, we perceive really present in the action of the Spirit who changes our faith community. "Grant that we, who are nourished by the Body and Blood of your Son and filled with his Holy Spirit, may become one body, one spirit in Christ" (Eucharistic Prayer III).

Unity and the Holy Spirit

Pope John Paul II urged Catholics to pray that the third millennium might be characterized by unity and peace. He said, "Among the most fervent petitions which the Church makes to the Lord during this important time...is that unity among all Christians...will increase until they reach full communion. I pray that [the new millennium] will be a promising opportunity for fruitful cooperation in the many areas which unite us; these are unquestionably more numerous than those which divide us."

It is the work of the Holy Spirit to ultimately fulfill the high priestly prayer of Jesus:

> I ask not only on behalf of these but also on behalf of those who will believe in me through their word, that they may all be one. As you, Father, are in me and I in you, may they also be in us, so that the world may believe that you have sent me. The glory that you have given me I have given them, so that they may be one, as we are one, I in them and you in me, that they may become completely one, so that the world may know that you have sent me and have loved them even as you have loved me. (John 17:20–23)

The courage and vision to strive for this ultimate unity are the promise and grace of confirmation, sacrament of the Spirit.

Canon 890 obliges the faithful to receive the sacrament of confirmation "at the proper time." It further decrees that pastors must take care to instruct the faithful about the sacrament and urge them to receive it at the appropriate time. Christian parents have the responsibility of seeing that their children are fully initiated.

Questions for Reflection

1. What does "laying on of hands" mean to you? Have you ever laid your hand on the head of a child? An adult? What did it mean?

2. What does anointing or "putting on oil" mean to you? When have you anointed your body (After a bath? On the beach? To soothe an itch?) What did it mean?

3. Which of the gifts of the Holy Spirit do you need most at this time in your life?

CHAPTER THREE

How Is Confirmation Administered?

In most U.S. Catholic parishes of the Latin Rite, confirmation is conferred either through the RCIA program or on children when they reach a selected age. Catholic parents recognize their special obligation to see that their children are baptized, confirmed, and receive First Communion. Part of the Rite of Baptism for Children is this reminder: "Dearly beloved, these children have been reborn in baptism. They are now called children of God, for so indeed they are. In confirmation they will receive the fullness of God's Spirit. In holy communion they will share the banquet of Christ's sacrifice."

At the Easter Vigil the newly baptized (also called "neophytes") who are to be confirmed are reminded, "Now you are to share in the outpouring of the Holy Spirit among us, the Spirit sent by the Lord upon his apostles at Pentecost and given by them and their successors to the baptized." Carol Luebering, Rita Burns Senseman, and Fr. Richstatter will explain.

Confirming Our Identity

Carol Luebering thinks of confirmation as an opportunity for young people to affirm their Christian identity. She writes: Preparation for confirmation includes learning to articulate what it means to be a Catholic Christian: the faith we express in Creed and lifestyle. Confirmation has long been delayed until a baptized infant could reach some understanding of these things—at least until the age of reason (about seven) and often until the approach of adolescence.

Today's confirmation candidates stand before a representative of the larger Church—the bishop or his delegate—and are anointed with the perfumed oil (chrism) blessed by the bishop at the Chrism Mass on Holy Thursday. They say with a knowledge and experience which they previously lacked as newly baptized infants, "Yes, this is my Church. I accept the faith of this Church as my faith. This is who I am."

Like the rest of us, today's confirmation candidate will continue to search for a better sense of divine reality until the day when eternal light explodes on newly opened eyes on the other side of the grave. Pledging faith to God is more a lifetime effort than a one-time action. It is therefore very difficult to speak of confirmation as a sacrament of "mature" commitment. As the *Catechism* warns, maturity in faith cannot be measured by age (see #1308).

Confirmation is the "seal" of God's promise. It marks us as God's property, a people set apart. In Catholic tradition confirmation is indeed a sacrament of commitment, but the commitment we celebrate was God's before it was ours. It is much less a sacrament of human commitment than a sacrament of faith in God's fidelity to us.

Using the RCIA

Rita Burns Senseman has long encouraged parish leaders in their use of the Rite of Christian Initiation of Adults. She explains: The RCIA is the Church's way of forming new disciples of Jesus Christ. It's the normative way the Catholic Church welcomes its newest members, but even more important than membership in the Catholic Church is discipleship in Christ Jesus. Through a gradual, complete and comprehensive training in the Christian way of life (Rite, # 75), the unbaptized come to know Jesus Christ through the Catholic Christian community and they learn to live as Jesus' disciples. Then, as disciples, they continue the mission of Jesus Christ in the world today.

Some people who participate in the RCIA are already disciples of Jesus Christ by virtue of their baptism in a Protestant denomination. Although the RCIA is designed primarily for the unbaptized, it can also be adapted for use with those who are already baptized, including adults and children over seven years of age.

Participating in the RCIA is much more than going to classes on Catholicism. It's undergoing a conversion to a new way of life in Christ. Although doctrinal instruction is a part of the formation process, the formation of disciples is more like an apprenticeship. The "apprentices" learn the Catholic Christian way of life from being in the midst of the parish community. The entire community helps form the apprentice in the Christian way of life.

At the Easter Vigil the members of the RCIA are invited to celebrate the Sacraments of Initiation: baptism (for those not yet baptized), confirmation, and Eucharist. The elect are plunged into the waters of new birth and come out of those waters reborn in Christ. They are then configured to be more like Christ through the sacred chrism of confirmation. Finally, the culmination of their initiation happens when they taste the Body and Blood of our Lord Jesus Christ in the Eucharist.

Confirmation Customs and Rules

Only the baptized can be confirmed. In the United States those to be confirmed (confirmandi) should be between the ages of seven and sixteen, though exceptions are possible.

Custom and Church law (Canon 892) strongly suggest that the person to be confirmed should have a sponsor, that is, a fully initiated Catholic to encourage and model Christian witness. Ideally the sponsor for confirmation is the baptismal sponsor or godparent of the one to be confirmed. The sponsor must be at least sixteen years old (exceptions are possible).

Whether the mother or father of the person to be confirmed can serve as a sponsor is moot since a strict reading of Canon 893 excludes a parent's serving in that role. But the Rite for Confirmation (paragraph 5) says, "Even the parents themselves may present their children for confirmation. It is for the local Ordinary [bishop] to determine diocesan practice in the light of local circumstances." A 1984 clarification from the Congregation for Divine Worship concerning the contradiction between canon law and rite conceded that parents may serve as confirmation sponsors for their children but not as baptism sponsors.

Canon 880 requires the use of chrism (in the Eastern Church it is called *myron*), a perfumed oil blessed by a bishop. It is in the act of anointing with this oil that the minister also imposes hands. Pope Paul VI described conferral of the sacrament in these terms: "The sacrament of confirmation is conferred through the anointing with chrism on the forehead which is done by the laying on of the hand, and through the words: Be sealed with the gift of the Holy Spirit."

The Three Elements of the Conferral

Fr. Richstatter, O.F.M. explains the significance of the anointing, the touch, and the words of the sacrament:

1. Anointing

What memories do you have of oil being applied to your body? I remember my mother rubbing Vick's Vapo-Rub on my chest when I was little and had a cold.

I remember the sensation of applying suntan lotion and lying on the beach in the Florida sun. And I remember the soothing ointment a doctor applied to my shoulder after a sports injury. Also, I like my popcorn "anointed" with butter.

Anointing can mean many things. From ancient times, oil has been a symbol of strength, healing, and agility. For Jews, our ancestors in the faith, oil is the sign of God appointing someone to be a priest, prophet and king.

Many Jews look forward to the time when a very special anointed one, a Hebrew messiah, will come to announce God's reign. The Hebrew word *messiah* means "anointed." It's a strong and important word.

Christians believe that Jesus of Nazareth was this anointed one. Our Christian Scriptures were written in the Greek language and "the Anointed One" is translated as "Christ" in Greek. Some of us are so used to speaking of "Jesus Christ" that "Christ" almost seems like Jesus' last name. We forget that it means Jesus, the

Anointed One, the Messiah.

As "Christ" means "anointed," we call ourselves "Christians" because we are the anointed ones, the "oiled people," so to speak. The sacraments of baptism, confirmation and Eucharist initiate us into that "oiled" community, the community anointed to continue the vocation of the Messiah, the Christ.

2. Touch

From ancient times, to impose hands on someone or to extend one's hand over the person's head was a sign of calling down the Holy Spirit. All seven sacraments employ this symbol. We call the prayer that accompanies the imposition of hands an *epiclesis*, which is an invocation.

At baptism, the priest lays his hand on those to be baptized and marks them with the sign of the cross. In the sacrament of reconciliation, the priest lays his hands on the head of the penitent and proclaims the words of absolution. During the anointing of the sick, the priest imposes hands on the person to be anointed.

In the sacrament of holy orders, the bishop imposes hands on the one to be ordained priest. During the sacrament of matrimony, the presider extends hands over the couple who have pronounced their wedding vows and calls the Holy Spirit upon them so that they may remain faithful to the marriage covenant.

In the sacrament of Eucharist, the priest invokes the Holy Spirit upon the gifts, extends his hands over the bread and wine and prays that the Holy Spirit change them into the Body and Blood of Christ so that we who receive them may be changed into that Body.

In confirmation, the presider places his hand on the head of each one to be confirmed and prays that the Holy Spirit descend upon them. You will hear the prayer to the Holy Spirit (see p. 26).

This prayer asks for the graces which we have come to call the seven gifts of the Holy Spirit. The number seven is itself a symbol of completeness, of boldness, of abundance. When we say that there are seven sacraments, we mean more than their number is one plus six. Seven sacraments implies the abundance of God's love for us and the all-sufficient nature of grace.

3. Words

The words used in the Rite are another symbol of confirmation. The words of the ceremony, the readings from Scripture, the homily, the invitation of the presider, the prayer for the sevenfold Spirit: all of these can help us learn the meaning of the sacrament.

When you are anointed, the presider first says your name and then says, "Be sealed with the gift of the Holy Spirit." Think about the significance of each of these words.

Your name: What does it mean to be called by name? In confirmation we hear again the name we were given in baptism. Confirmation begins with baptism. (Some people take a new name at confirmation in order to have an additional heavenly patron.)

Seal: This word has a rich meaning in our religion. In earlier times a document was shown to be authentic by the author putting his seal on the document (often with a signet ring) in a spot of hot wax. This distinctive mark or seal was like the person's signature. In confirmation we receive God's mark, God's seal. God permanently and eternally seals us as God's anointed ones.

We receive the sacrament of confirmation only once. What happens to us in confirmation so conforms us to Christ that the sacrament can never be repeated. We speak of this special conformity to Christ as the sacramental character of confirmation.

Gift: This is a key word in the sacrament of confirmation. It reminds us that we are celebrating God's work. Sometimes we prepare for confirmation by years of study and service and it may seem that confirmation is a reward, something we have earned.

But confirmation is not our work. It is God's gift. And what is that gift? The Holy Spirit is God's first gift to those who believe.

When you think of the word *spirit,* what comes to mind? School spirit? Team spirit? When we speak of "team spirit," for example, we are referring to something that the members of the team possess and also something that is beyond the individual members. It is something that they all share, something that energizes them, something that gives them a common goal and vision.

That is what God's Spirit does to us. The Holy Spirit is God's breath in us. God's breath gives our bodies a special (divine) life, energy, and enthusiasm. The Spirit makes us not only like the members of a team, but also makes us much more. We become the members of one body, Christ's body. The Holy Spirit unites us in the body of Christ so that, with him, we can call God our Father—actually "Abba," which is more like daddy. It is this Holy Spirit that gives us our identity, that tells us who we are: the body of Christ.

St. Paul uses this analogy with the human body to describe our relation with Christ. St. John uses a different analogy, that of a vine and its branches. At the Last Supper Jesus says to the disciples, "I am the vine, you are the branches. Those who abide in me and I in them bear much fruit, because apart from you can do nothing" (John 15:5). In this analogy, the Holy Spirit can be compared to the sap of the plant, giving life to both vine and branches

Confirmation and Baptism

Every confirmation begins with baptism. This is true whether the baptism was celebrated only a few moments before confirmation (as in many Eastern Rites and in the RCIA), whether the baptism was celebrated six years before (as in those dioceses where confirmation is celebrated before First Communion), fourteen years before confirmation, or even fifty years before confirmation.

Confirmation complements the symbols of baptism. Confirmation means all that baptism means.

The historical origins of the symbols of confirmation are many and diverse. One source of the rituals for the sacrament of confirmation can be found in the bathing customs of the Roman Empire. After a bath, Romans applied bath oil. In our times, when you take a shower, you wash up and dry off. In Roman times, oil was a part of the bathing ritual. A bath included both water and oil.

Today, if a friend asked you to go to a movie and you said, "Sure. But don't come by until 6 PM because I want to take a shower first," I suspect that by shower you include not only the washing up but also the drying off. Drying off is understood to be part of the total shower. In the same way, the early Church saw confirmation as a part of the baptism experience.

The water ritual (baptism) came to mean the washing away of sin, and the oil ritual (confirmation) was interpreted to mean the sweet fragrance of God's presence: sanctifying grace.

We know that sin cannot be removed except by grace, just as, for example, a vacuum cannot be removed from a container without replacing it (the emptiness) with something. The two go together. In the same way God's grace fills us with redemption and salvation. This grace, this presence of God in us, is the Holy Spirit. Confirmation is the sacrament of the Holy Spirit.

Confirmation and Eucharist

The final and most important symbol of confirmation is Eucharist. Eucharist is the fullness of confirmation and the completion of Christian initiation. In baptism our sins are washed away; in confirmation we are filled with the Holy Spirit. This Spirit empowers us to continue Christ's messianic (anointed) vocation. The life of Christ was first and foremost a life praising God.

Our praise of God culminates in the Eucharist. The Eucharist is the repeatable part of confirmation. In each Eucharist the Holy Spirit comes upon us anew to strengthen us for service. Filled with Christ's spirit and united in his body we can fulfill in our lives the command of Christ: Do this in memory of me. We can live our lives as Christ lived his. As St. Paul wrote in his Second Letter to the Corinthians (5:18), we continue Christ's ministry of reconciliation and serve as agents of healing in this broken world. This is the ministry of confirmation; this is the ministry of Christianity.

Questions for Reflection

1. How can the reception of confirmation be an opportunity for personally accepting your identity as a Christian?

2. If you were asked to be a confirmation sponsor, what would you be expected to do?

3. Although confirmation is received only once, in what way is your going to Communion (receiving the Eucharist) "the repeatable part of confirmation"?

What Does It All Mean?

In the earliest years of Christianity, baptism and confirmation were closely united, and generally conferred in the same ceremony on the same occasion. The convert was baptized and then hands were laid upon him.

It is likely that a sharper distinction was drawn between the two sides of the same coin, baptism and confirmation, when it was decided that bishops were the usual ministers of the imposition of hands. A deacon or elder might baptize, but the bishop was the proper minister for confirming what baptism began.

It is not clear when oil became part of this ritual action, but by the start of the third century the North African theologian Tertullian was writing about a post-baptismal anointing.

Although we cannot be sure whether this oil was used as part of the baptizing or part of the laying on of hands, we do know that in the fifth-century Church leadership insisted that the bishop was to "finish" the baptism ceremony by imposing hands.

The New Testament explicitly states that Jesus sent his disciples to baptize, but there is nothing in the Gospels to indicate that Jesus called for the laying on of hands or the anointing with oil in the ritual action that we now call confirmation. The great thirteenth-century theologian Thomas Aquinas, however, suggested that Jesus did institute confirmation by his promise to send the Holy Spirit. Aquinas implied that Jesus let the Church decide what would be used to signify the granting and coming of that Spirit.

Today the Roman Church legislates that the sign of confirmation is both the anointing with chrism and the laying on of hands in a simultaneous gesture. (It is noteworthy that the Eastern Churches call this sacrament "chrismation.") Since Jesus did not stipulate what would be the sign of the conferral of the Holy Spirit, the Church has at various times focused on the imposition of hands and then on the anointing with oil. The Church's current practice combines them into one sign or gesture of grace: laying hands while anointing.

The separation of the confirmation ritual from the baptism ritual has contributed to differing interpretations about confirmation. What is it? How is to be done? When is it to be conferred?

Sacrament of Initiation or Sacrament of Maturity?

There can be no doubt that at this time in its history the Church considers confirmation to be one of the three Sacraments of Initiation. The *Catechism of the Catholic Church* says clearly, "Christian initiation is accomplished by three sacraments together: Baptism which is the beginning of new life; Confirmation which is its strengthening; and the Eucharist, which nourishes the disciple with Christ's Body and Blood for his transformation in Christ" (#1275).

Without denying that confirmation is part of the initiation process, there are Catholics who speak of confirmation as "the sacrament of maturity." In this understanding, confirmation is reserved to a time after the age of discretion (which is about age seven) so that young people may have matured enough to make a personal choice to be confirmed. Some think of confirmation as a rite of passage, an occasion marking a deeper formation in Gospel values than expected of a second grader.

In addition confirmation becomes the occasion for encouraging the *confirmandi* to give witness to the Gospel by their words and actions, and to bear with the ridicule and rejection that may come to those who truly live a Christian life. The confirmed are expected to use their various gifts for building up God's holy people.

The age at which young people are confirmed in the United States varies from diocese to diocese, and even from parish to parish in a given diocese. Some pastors and parish directors of religious formation, especially those with religious education programs for children who do not attend Catholic schools, want to delay confirmation as a way of keeping in touch with these children. Many catechists know that once some young people are confirmed, they stop attending the parish program for religious instruction.

One consequence of this age variation is that many young Catholics end up not being confirmed. If a youngster moves from a parish where confirmation is conferred at age fifteen to a parish where the age for receiving the sacrament is age twelve, that young Catholic may miss formal preparation for and reception of confirmation. Many pastors preparing couples for marriage discover that the future bride or groom has never been confirmed.

Gift or Gifts of the Holy Spirit?

Another variation in interpreting confirmation is whether the focus of the sacrament is the reception of the *gift* of the Holy Spirit, or the reception of the many gifts with which the Holy Spirit empowers the one who is confirmed.

The official Rite for Confirmation includes a sample homily for the occasion. It includes this statement: "Bishops are successors of the Apostles and have this power of giving the Holy Spirit to the baptized, either personally or through the priests they appoint.... You have already been baptized into Christ and now you will receive the power of his Spirit and the sign of the cross on your forehead" (see #22).

One might conclude from this homily that the Holy Spirit is not given until confirmation. But if baptism is a new birth by water and the Spirit, it would be incongruous to say that the Spirit is not given in baptism. It is more accurate to say that confirmation brings a fuller expression of the Spirit in the initiated Christian's life.

Other interpreters of the sacrament focus on the gifts that the Spirit makes manifest in the life of a fully initiated Christian. As we see in chapter two of the Acts of the Apostles, Jesus sent the Spirit upon the Church at Pentecost, and with that Spirit came special gifts, most notably the gift of their being able to speak in a variety of languages. In his sermon that day, Peter tied their Pentecost experience to the prophecy of Joel, who said that God would pour out his spirit, manifesting itself in such gifts as visions, prophecies, and wonders in the heavens.

Confirmation is an expression of Pentecost. In the Rite's sample homily we hear the preacher say, "Christ gives varied gifts to his Church, and the Spirit distributes them among the members of Christ's body to build up the holy people of God in unity and love."

E Pluribus Unum

As much as we might like to resolve the conflicts in interpretation of the sacrament of confirmation, we have before us a mystery to be explored, with theologies not so much contradictory as multi-faceted. Out of the many practices and understandings applicable to confirmation comes one shining reality, namely, the assurance that we belong to God. If the mark placed on Cain was a sign both of his failure and of God's mercy, so the mark placed on us in confirmation is a sign both of our choosing God and of God's choosing us:

"Be sealed with the gift of the Holy Spirit."

Sources

Most of the information in this book comes from:

Luebering, Carol. "Confirmation: A Deepening of Our Christian Identity." *Catholic Update,* October 1995.

Martos, Joseph. "What Difference Does Confirmation Make?" *Youth Update,* March 1985.

Richstatter, Thomas, O.F.M. "Seven Symbols in One Sacrament." *Youth Update,* April 1997.

———. "Sacraments of Initiation: Sacraments of Invitation." *Catholic Update,* March 2001.

———. "Confirmation: Sacrament of the Spirit." *Millennium Monthly,* August 1998.

Senseman, Rita Burns, "A New Look at the RCIA: Journey for the Entire Parish." *Catholic Update,* May 2002.

Contributors

Carol Luebering was a prolific author and editor at St. Anthony Messenger Press. Her books include *Coping With Loss: Praying Your Way to Acceptance* and *Handing on the Faith* titles.

Norm Langenbrunner has served as a high school teacher, associate pastor, and parish pastor. He has written articles for *Liguorian, The Bible Today, St Anthony Messenger,* and *Catechist.*

Joseph Martos is a retired professor of philosophy and theology and author of *Doors to the Sacred: A Historical Introduction to Sacraments in the Church,* and *The Sacraments: An Interdisciplinary and Interactive Study.*

Thomas Richstatter, O.F.M., has a doctorate in sacramental theology from Institut Catholique of Paris, and is currently a faculty member at St. Meinrad School of Theology. He is the author of *The Mass: A Guided Tour.*

Rita Burns Senseman is a catechist focusing on the Christian initiation of children. She is a team member for the North American Forum on the Catechumenate, and the author of *Handing on the Faith: When You Are an RCIA Sponsor.*

Your monthly publication
committed to adult faith formation from
St. Anthony Messenger Press

Call 1-800-488-0488 **for a FREE sample.**

- Explore Catholic tradition
- Understand the sacraments
- Explain Church teaching
- Encourage seasonal renewal

www.CatholicUpdate.com